BRITISH
WARSHIPS
AND AUXILIARIES

HMS Beaver

THE ROYAL NAVY

Each year we intend to invite a well respected and informed defence journalist to introduce this book as a "guest author" - outlining how they see the current naval scene. This year we welcome Antony Preston to provide our introduction.

As 1996 drew to a close the Royal Navy was in an interesting state. Too small for its tasks, that goes without saying, but in better shape than it has been for some years. It can be claimed with considerable justification that the Navy has faced the realities of the post-Cold War world better than its sister services, the Army and the Royal Air Force.

Justifying such a claim might seem a waste of time, but before the supporters of a strong Royal Navy denounce me as a defeatist or worse still, an apologist for the Treasury and the Ministry of Defence, it is well to look at some facts. The Army seemed to get bogged down in a sterile argument about which regiment should merge with which, while the RAF, *which spent more money on the Tornado programme than the Navy spent on Trident* (a fact the RAF is understandably reluctant to publicise), has ended up with an air defence fighter with dismal performance.

Looking for a New Mission

The Navy, it must be said, nearly fell into the trap of trying to pretend that the Soviet Navy was still there, red in tooth and claw as well as ideology. Before long the dramatic evidence of a catastrophic collapse of the Russian Navy's infrastructure was impossible to hide, and it was clear that the Russians cannot afford to restart the Cold War, even if they wish to. This in turn led to a mood of complacency among the public and opinion-formers, summarised by the question, "Where is the Threat".

Fortunately the Navy stopped trying to win that argument, and concentrated its energy on defining a new role. In the process it rediscovered its principal advantage - flexibility. While others made laborious plans to create rapid-reaction forces, the Navy reminded its political masters that it has always been a rapid-reaction force. It has rightly seen that its best policy for the late 1990s and the early years of the next century is to recreate a modest out-of-area capability, built around the Royal Marines and amphibious ships.

The magnitude of this victory for common sense should not be overlooked. In 1981 John Nott's civil service advisers tried to axe the amphibious capability (and wanted to get rid of the Royal Marines at the same time). The justification for this idiocy was the claim that the Royal Navy's only role was that of an anti-submarine force confined to the waters off North Western Europe. Despite the ample proof provided by the recovery of the Falklands a year later, Mr Nott's advisers tried to implement the same policy as soon as they felt that the coast was clear, and it was politically safe to do so. They tried "benign neglect", putting off the replacements for the amphibious dock transports HMS FEARLESS and HMS INTREPID, possibly hoping that the ships would have to be withdrawn without being replaced.

To its credit the Navy fought the case for the amphibious forces, and headed off an attempt by the nuclear submarine lobby to delete the proposed Auxiliary Support Ship (ASS), later to become the amphibious assault helicopter carrier OCEAN. Finding the money to build the replacements for the FEARLESS and INTREPID proved much harder, but in 1996 the ALBION and BULWARK were ordered. It is scandalous that the "urgent" need for these ships was publicly admitted in 1983, a mere 14 years ago! Which makes it all the more satisfying that all three ships have been procured at very modest prices.

Modernising the Fleet

Despite dismal predictions, the Navy will get all 16 "Duke" class anti-submarine frigates, the total originally planned. The gamble on their new DNA(1) command system has paid off, and all the ships at sea now have a major part of the software working. The system is expected to reach full functionality by the end of 1997 and the last ships will receive the full system on completion. The Navy now has a command system suitable for the next century and widely admitted to be as good as anything in any other front-line navy. Equally gratifying is the knowledge that the "Duke" class remain relatively cheap, especially when compared with equivalent designs in other navies.

It is always sad to see fine old warships going out of service, but it is also essential for the Royal Navy to rid itself of ships with large complements and non-standard equipment. Personnel costs account for over half the annual budget, so the Navy must learn how to run its ships with fewer people. Maintenance of elderly equipment, particularly weapons and electronics, is also expensive. Introducing modern systems with a high degree of commonality is the only way to ensure a high state of readiness at a price which is affordable. That was the reason for taking the Leander class out of service and for selling the four Broadsword class (Type 22 Batch 1) to Brazil.

The Royal Fleet Auxiliary was also a victim of the "John Nott Syndrome", the belief that the Navy would never àgain operate out-of-area. Now at last the two Fort Victoria class AORs are to be supplemented by two new large oilers (AOs), to be in service by 2000 This goes some way to make good the deficiencies of the RFA, which now has only three very old replenishment ships in service. Two of the RFA's four oldest logistic landing ships (LSLs) have undergone major modernisation, although SIR BEDIVERE will be a year late by the time her refit is completed. There is now some doubt that even one of the remaining pair will be brought up to the same standard, and it might be more cost-effective to build new LSLs.

The launch of the ocean survey vessel SCOTT last year is a major step in the process of revitalising the hydrographic fleet. She will provide much-needed data of the seabed and the whole marine environment. A new oceanographic survey ship is planned as replacement for HMS HERALD, and two hydrographic survey vessels to replace the BEAGLE and BULLDOG.

The order for seven more Sandown class minehunters in 1994, however long delayed, will provide a welcome reinforcement for the mine countermeasures (MCM) forces. The first, to be named

3

PENZANCE, should be delivered at the end of the year, and the last, SHOREHAM, will join the fleet in 2001. Hopes of a major upgrade for the 13 "Hunt" class are fading, and it is rumoured that they will receive little more than a refurbishment.

On the submarine front the situation is not so straightforward. The case for maintaining the nuclear deterrent is one for the politicians, and the Navy had no option but to implement the national policy. What cannot be taken seriously is the argument that we could have had a much bigger navy if Trident had been cancelled. Once the costing of Trident and the new SSBNs had been done, and the Navy had conceded that it could live with a smaller surface fleet, there was no way that the Treasury would have "refunded" the money. Many naval officers and supporters of the Navy have peddled this argument, but they forget that the decision to be a nuclear power is not one over which the Armed Forces have any say. The third of the Vanguard class, HMS VIGILANT, was commissioned last November, and the final vessel, the VENGEANCE, is planned for delivery at the end of 1998 or early in 1999.

The scaling-down of the SSN force to ten boats makes sense in the post-Cold War period. SSNs are very potent but they have only a relatively small part to play in peacekeeping or littoral operations. The acquisition of Tomahawk cruise missiles goes some way to remedy that problem, but the fact remains that submarines gain most from concealment, not from an overt display of their presence. As the Falklands conflict showed, they can intervene with devastating effect, but unlike other elements of sea power, submarines have to attack ships, and that means a "hot" war. The other submarine roles of surveillance and insertion of SBS units are very valuable for specific circumstances, but they are peripheral activities. The news that the Batch 2 Trafalgar class (B2TC) will go ahead, as well as the upgrade of the surviving Swiftsures and the current Trafalgar class, is very reassuring to the submariners, who seemed at one stage to be facing serious cuts in strength.

The saga of the Upholder class conventional submarines has now achieved the stage of low comedy. The Navy's case for taking them out of service had some validity; a separate support organisation for only four SSKs would have been uneconomical, and at a time of severe financial constraint was not justified. But since then, the efforts to sell them have become an embarrassment. Clearly any potential customer merely has to "sit on his hands" until the price comes down. Only the Treasury seems to labour under the delusion that these boats can be sold for anything like their original cost. It would be better to give them to a foreign navy as part of a package which includes a binding promise to buy new warships from British shipyards. As it is, the sorry sight of the Upholders being flogged around the bazaars by an ever-more desperate band of Defence Export Services salesmen does nothing to persuade anyone to even think of buying a British diesel-electric submarine design in the future.

Who would buy an SSK from a country whose navy does not appear to have any faith in the very idea?

Winning Future Battles

The next procurement problem to be solved is the "Horizon" Common New-Generation Frigate (CNGF), the powerful air defence design intended to replace the Type 42 BIRMINGHAM and MANCHESTER class destroyers in the early years of the next century. This very ambitious programme is a partnership with France and Italy to economise on cost and to foster European col-

4

laboration. The aim is very worthy, but it has proved very hard to achieve, and we will not see any of the three navies' first-of-class ships until 2004. The Royal Navy is officially still committed to building a dozen "Horizons", but as time passes it seems less and less likely that the Navy will be able to afford more than eight.

Turning to other matters, the real risk the Navy faces is over-stretch. Not in the individual sense, but in the overall sense, that Jack cannot be asked to make continual sacrifices of time and effort, just to compensate for a cash-strapped MoD's failure to make its case properly. Time and time again Jack has risen magnificently to the occasion, but if emergencies become a habit the men and women at the "sharp end" are entitled to ask, "what has this got to do with patriotism?". Put another way, "if the country doesn't seem to care, why should we?". The politicians and the civil servants must never be allowed to take service people for granted.

In a less obvious way, the argument applies to the ships as well. One of the best things to come out of the 1987 House of Commons Defence Committee enquiry into the size and shape of the future Fleet was the admission that warships have a finite life. A worn-out ship is not only expensive to run but frustrating to all who serve in her. The cynics might say that everyone loves a "dock-yard limpet", but in practice nobody likes to be associated with a lame duck. It goes without saying that unreliable weapons are bad for morale, particularly when there is a risk that they might have to be used in anger.

One of the problems with a tradition-rich service like the Royal Navy is the way in which "sacred cows" proliferate. The row over the closure of Portland and the equally vituperative debate over the future of the Royal Naval College in Greenwich are only the latest examples of the manufacture of spurious traditions. Portland did not assume any significance as a major base until the period before the First World War, when the Channel and Home Fleets became so large that it was necessary to provide some "overflow" capacity. This led to the torpedo boat and destroyer base at Portland being expanded to handle a battle squadron and its supporting cruisers. In 1914-18 it assumed considerable importance as a base for escorts but it declined in importance immediately after the Armistice. Then came the Second World War, when the importance of coastal shipping and the battle to contain German light forces brought Portland back into prominence. Instead of allowing it to decline once more, the Admiralty made it the home of the Training Squadron after 1945, and eventually FOST's organisation was based there. By the 1980s it was clear that the shrunken Royal Navy had too much dockyard capacity, but Portland survived because of its importance to the local economy. Similarly, the Navy cannot seriously claim that it has been associated with Greenwich for "centuries". Wren's masterpiece was not built for the Navy, but for naval pensioners, and the College did not function as such until after the middle of the last century. Part of our maritime heritage, yes, but an indispensable element of the Navy's heritage, no. Its functions really can be replicated by a rented office block in Basingstoke. Nor is it right that the Navy should be chastised for extravagance while the naval budget has to bear the cost of keeping up a national architectural asset.

Progress Since 1982

Looking back to the Falklands conflict 15 years ago, it is interesting to compare the state of the Navy then and now. The Navy is smaller but more flexible than it was then, and despite the dramatic recasting of its role after the collapse of the Soviet Union, it is better equipped. Since 1982 the Navy has handled a number of crises very efficiently, culminating in the Gulf War and the operations off Bosnia. There is no longer any sterile debate about the design of ships, with cranks peddling their nostrums and shaking public confidence in the Navy's materiel. New weapons, systems and procedures are in place to prevent a recurrence of the problems encountered.

Public Perceptions of Maritime Matters

The transfer of British Merchant Navy ships to foreign-flag registration has not proved the disaster predicted. The real threat is that the shrinkage in the merchant fleet and the closure of shipyards is fostering the collapse of the infrastructure, in the form of training facilities and the myriad services required by a vigorous merchant fleet. Despite stalwart efforts by various pressure-groups, the British public seems to have completely forgotten that freight travels by sea, not by air. As an American naval analyst has said, "they must learn that you cannot transport crude oil in Boeing 747s". This nonsense is actively promoted by air power lobbyists, who forget that 95 per cent of the war materiel needed for the Gulf War went to Saudi Arabia by sea, not by air.

Even the recent uproar over a TV documentary series on HMS BRILLIANT has had no serious effect. I recall a similar fuss made about "Sailor", and when I spent some time aboard the old Ark Royal in 1978 I found the ship's company divided roughly on age lines. Older officers and ratings all wondered "what the Navy is coming to", whereas the younger people said, "if the public doesn't like the Navy they have, then they had better go out and buy themselves a different one". Luckily I was able to tell the pessimists that I had just returned from Sweden, where "Sailor" was top of the TV ratings. The opinion of everyone I met was that the documentary proved that we still had the best navy in the world, even if not the biggest. When I asked what they thought of the rowdy scenes in Diamond Lil's, the reply was, "even supermen have to have some time off". As they say in the courts, I rest my case.

Antony Preston

London
December, 1996

6

SHIPS OF THE ROYAL NAVY
Pennant Numbers

Ship	Pennant Number	Ship	Pennant Number
Aircraft Carriers		COVENTRY	F98
		CORNWALL	F99
INVINCIBLE	R05 ✓	LANCASTER	F229
ILLUSTRIOUS	R06 ✓	NORFOLK	F230
ARK ROYAL ●	R07 ✓	ARGYLL	F231 ✓
		MARLBOROUGH	F233 ✓
Destroyers		IRON DUKE	F234 ✓ 23 5 98
		MONMOUTH	F235 ✓
BIRMINGHAM	D86 ✓	MONTROSE	F236
NEWCASTLE	D87 ✓	WESTMINSTER	F237
GLASGOW	D88 ✓	NORTHUMBERLAND	F238
EXETER	D89 ✓	RICHMOND	F239
SOUTHAMPTON	D90 ✓		
NOTTINGHAM	D91 ✓	**Submarines**	
LIVERPOOL	D92 ✓		
MANCHESTER	D95 ✓	VANGUARD	S28
GLOUCESTER	D96 ✓	VICTORIOUS	S29
EDINBURGH	D97	VIGILANT	S30
YORK	D98	UPHOLDER ●	S40
CARDIFF	D108 ✓	UNSEEN ●	S41
		URSULA ●	S42
Frigates		UNICORN ●	S43
		TRENCHANT	S91
GRAFTON	F80	TALENT	S92
SUTHERLAND	F81	TRIUMPH	S93
SOMERSET	F82	SCEPTRE	S104
CUMBERLAND	F85	SPARTAN	S105
CAMPBELTOWN	F86	SPLENDID	S106
CHATHAM	F87	TRAFALGAR	S107
BATTLEAXE	F89 ✓	SOVEREIGN	S108
BOXER	F92 ✓	SUPERB	S109
BEAVER	F93	TURBULENT	S110
BRAVE	F94	TIRELESS	S117
LONDON	F95 ✓	TORBAY	S118
SHEFFIELD	F96		

Ship	Pennant Number	Ship	Pennant Number
Assault Ships		DUMBARTON CASTLE	P265
		BITER	P270
FEARLESS	L10 ✓	SMITER	P272
INTREPID ●	L11 ✓	PURSUER	P273 ✓
OCEAN	L12	ANGLESEY	P277 ✓ 23592
		ALDERNEY	P278
Minesweepers & Minehunters		BLAZER	P279 ✓
		DASHER	P280 ✓
		PUNCHER	P291 ✓
BRECON	M29	CHARGER	P292
LEDBURY	M30 ✓	RANGER	P293
CATTISTOCK	M31 ✓	TRUMPETER	P294
COTTESMORE	M32 ✓	GUERNSEY	P297
BROCKLESBY	M33 ✓	SHETLAND	P298
MIDDLETON	M34 ✓	ORKNEY	P299
DULVERTON	M35 ✓	LINDISFARNE	P300
BICESTER	M36		
CHIDDINGFOLD	M37	**Survey Ships & RN Manned Auxiliaries**	
ATHERSTONE	M38 ✓		
HURWORTH	M39 ✓	BRITANNIA	A00
BERKELEY	M40	GLEANER	A86
QUORN	M41	ROEBUCK	A130
SANDOWN	M101 ✓	SCOTT	A131
INVERNESS	M102	HERALD	A138
CROMER	M103	LOYAL WATCHER	A159
WALNEY	M104	EXPRESS	(P) A163 ✓
BRIDPORT	M105	EXPLORER	A164
BLACKWATER	M2008	EXAMPLE	A165
ITCHEN	M2009	EXPLOIT	(P) A167 ✓
ORWELL	M2011 ✓	ENDURANCE	A171 ✓
SPEY	M2013	IRONBRIDGE	A311
ARUN	M2014 ✓	BULLDOG	A317 ✓
		IXWORTH	A318
Patrol Craft		BEAGLE	A319 ✓
PEACOCK	P239	LOYAL CHANCELLOR	A1770
PLOVER	P240		
STARLING	P241		
LEEDS CASTLE	P258		
ARCHER	P264	● *Ships in reserve/long refit*	

8

KEEP UP TO DATE
THROUGHOUT THE YEAR

Warship World is published each quarter and gives you all the information necessary to keep this book updated throughout the year. See inside front cover for details.

This book is updated and re-issued every *December*. Keep up to date … Don't miss the new edition.

Phone 01579 343663 for details.

HMS Victorious

VANGUARD CLASS

Ship	Pennant Number	Completion Date	Builder
VANGUARD	S28	1992	VSEL
VICTORIOUS	S29	1994	VSEL
VIGILANT	S30	1996	VSEL
VENGEANCE	S31		VSEL

Displacement 15,000 tons (dived) **Dimensions** 150m x 13m x 12m **Speed** 25 + dived **Armament** 16 - Trident 2 (D5) missiles, 4 Torpedo Tubes **Complement** 135 (2 crews).

Notes

The completion date of VENGEANCE (due 1998) has been put back. VIGILANT & VENGEANCE are now officially described as "entering service in the next few years"

● HMS NEPTUNE

HMS Sceptre

SWIFTSURE CLASS

Ship	Pennant Number	Completion Date	Builder
SCEPTRE	S104	1978	Vickers
SPARTAN	S105	1979	Vickers
SPLENDID	S106	1980	Vickers
SOVEREIGN	S108	1974	Vickers
SUPERB	S109	1976	Vickers

Displacement 4,500 tons dived **Dimensions** 83m x 10m x 8m **Speed** 30 knots + dived **Armament** 5 Torpedo Tubes **Complement** 116.

Notes
All are based at Faslane. SWIFTSURE is awaiting disposal at Rosyth. The class will be replaced in due course by the Batch 2 Trafalgar class boats.

● D HANNAFORD

HMS Triumph

TRAFALGAR CLASS

Ship	Pennant Number	Completion Date	Builder
TRENCHANT	S91	1989	Vickers
TALENT	S92	1990	Vickers
TRIUMPH	S93	1991	Vickers
TRAFALGAR	S107	1983	Vickers
TURBULENT	S110	1984	Vickers
TIRELESS	S117	1985	Vickers
TORBAY	S118	1986	Vickers

Displacement 4,500 tons **Dimensions** 85m x 10m x 8m **Speed** 30 + dived **Armament** 5 Torpedo Tubes **Complement** 125.

Notes

Enhanced development of the Swiftsure Class. Quieter, faster and with greater endurance than their predecessors. Tomahawk Cruise Missiles may eventually be fitted in these boats. Three new, Batch 2, Trafalgar Class were expected to be ordered in early 1996 and a further two at a later date.but no orders were placed by the end of '96.

● MARITIME PHOTOGRAPHIC

HMS Unicorn

UPHOLDER CLASS

Ship	Pennant Number	Completion Date	Builder
UPHOLDER	S40	1989	Vickers
UNSEEN	S41	1991	Cammell Laird
URSULA	S42	1992	Cammell Laird
UNICORN	S43	1993	Cammell Laird

Displacement 2,400 tons (dived) **Dimensions** 70m x 8m x 5m **Speed** 20 knots dived **Armament** 6 Torpedo Tubes: Sub Harpoon missile **Complement** 44.

Notes
A new class of conventionally powered submarines. As a result of Defence economies announced in 1993 all the class have been actively marketed for sale/lease overseas. They were paid off during 1994 and remain laid up at Barrow-in-Furness.

HMS Illustrious

INVINCIBLE CLASS

Ship	Pennant Number	Completion Date	Builder
INVINCIBLE	R05	1979	Vickers
ILLUSTRIOUS	R06	1982	Swan Hunter
ARK ROYAL	R07	1985	Swan Hunter

Displacement 19,500 tons **Dimensions** 206m x 32m x 6.5m **Speed** 28 knots **Armament** Sea Dart Missile, 2 - 20mm guns, 3 Phalanx/Goalkeeper **Aircraft** 8 - Sea Harrier, 12 - Sea King **Complement** 900 + aircrews.

Notes

Manpower problems have dictated that only two ships are kept in the operational fleet, with the third in refit or reserve. ARK ROYAL is in reserve at Portsmouth but is due to be refitted at Rosyth in 1998.

14

HMS Ocean

OCEAN

Ship	Pennant Number	Completion Date	Builder
OCEAN	L12	1998	Kvaerner

Displacement 20,000 tons **L.O.A.** 203m **Speed** 19 knots **Complement** Ship 258, Squadrons 180, Embarked force 800.

Notes
Launched in October 1995 at Kvaerner's yard in Glasgow. Sailed November 1996 for fitting out at Barrow during 1997. Provisional acceptance due in Spring 1998.

OFFICIAL PHOTO

HMS Fearless

FEARLESS CLASS

Ship	Pennant Number	Completion Date	Builder
FEARLESS	L10	1965	Harland & Wolff
INTREPID	L11	1967	J. Brown

Displacement 12,500 tons, 19,500 tons (flooded) **Dimensions** 158m x 24m x 8m **Speed** 20 knots **Armament** 2 - Vulcan Phalanx (FEARLESS only) 2 - 40mm guns, 4 - 30mm **Complement** 580.

Notes
Multi-purpose ships that can operate helicopters for embarked Royal Marine Commandos. 4 landing craft are carried on an internal deck and are flooded out when the ship docks down. INTREPID paid off at Portsmouth in 1991 when a decision was made that both vessels would be replaced. Financial restraints delayed any order being made until 1996 when it was announced that two new vessels were to be ordered and named ALBION & BULWARK.FEARLESS is to be kept operational until 2002/3 when the first vessel is expected to be delivered.It was reported to Parliament in 1996 that £32 million had been spent on INTREPID's maintenance since she paid off.

HMS Southampton

SHEFFIELD CLASS
(Type 42) Batch 1 & 2

Ship	Pennant Number	Completion Date	Builder
BIRMINGHAM	D86	1976	C. Laird
NEWCASTLE	D87	1978	Swan Hunter
GLASGOW	D88	1978	Swan Hunter
EXETER	D89	1980	Swan Hunter
SOUTHAMPTON	D90	1981	Vosper T.
NOTTINGHAM	D91	1982	Vosper T.
LIVERPOOL	D92	1982	C. Laird
CARDIFF	D108	1979	Vickers

Displacement 3,660 tons **Dimensions** 125m x 15m x 7m **Speed** 29 knots **Armament** 1 - 4.5" gun, 4 - 20mm guns, Sea Dart Missile System: 2 - Phalanx, Lynx Helicopter, 6 Torpedo Tubes **Complement** 280 +.

Notes
Sister Ships SHEFFIELD and COVENTRY lost in 1982 during the Falklands conflict. The first of class for disposal will be BIRMINGHAM in 1998.

● OFFICIAL PHOTO

HMS Gloucester

SHEFFIELD CLASS
(Type 42) Batch 3

Ship	Pennant Number	Completion Date	Builder
MANCHESTER	D95	1983	Vickers
GLOUCESTER	D96	1984	Vosper T.
EDINBURGH	D97	1985	C. Laird
YORK	D98	1984	Swan Hunter

Displacement 4,775 tons **Dimensions** 132m x 15m x 7m **Speed** 30 knots + **Armament** 1- 4.5" gun, 1- Phalanx, 4 - 20mm guns. Sea Dart missile system. Lynx Helicopter, 6 Torpedo Tubes **Complement** 301.

Notes

"Stretched' versions of earlier ships of this class. Designed to provide area defence of a task force. Deck edge stiffening fitted to counter increased hull stress. Studies continue (with France and Italy) on the requirement for a Common New Generation Frigate to enter service in 2004.

18

● OFFICIAL PHOTO

HMS Battleaxe

BROADSWORD CLASS
(Type 22) Batch 1

Ship	Pennant Number	Completion Date	Builder
BATTLEAXE	F89	1980	Yarrow

Displacement 3,860 tons **Dimensions** 131m x 15m x 6m **Speed** 29 knots **Armament** 4 Exocet Missiles, 2 Sea Wolf Missile Systems, 4 - 30mm guns, 2 or 4 - 20mm guns, 6 Torpedo Tubes, 2 Lynx Helicopters **Complement** 224.

Notes
Although capable of carrying 2 helicopters, only 1 normally embarked. BROADSWORD sold to Brazil in 1995. BRAZEN and BRILLIANT in 1996. BATTLEAXE will also be transferred on 30 April 1997 to complete a £100 million deal.

19

● L/AIR C LEASK

HMS Beaver

BROADSWORD CLASS
(Type 22) Batch 2

Ship	Pennant Number	Completion Date	Builder
BOXER	F92	1983	Yarrow
BEAVER	F93	1984	Yarrow
BRAVE•	F94	1985	Yarrow
LONDON •	F95	1986	Yarrow
SHEFFIELD •	F96	1987	Swan Hunter
COVENTRY •	F98	1988	Swan Hunter

Displacement 4,100 tons **Dimensions** 143m x 15m x 6m **Speed** 30 knots **Armament** 4 Exocet Missiles, 2 Sea Wolf Missile Systems, 4 - 30mm + 2 - 20mm guns, 6 Torpedo Tubes, 2 Lynx Helicopters **Complement** 273.

Notes
• Ships have enlarged hangar and flight deck. A Sea King can be, and is, carried in some ships of this class. All ships have an intelligence gathering capability.

20

● OFFICIAL PHOTO

HMS Chatham

BROADSWORD CLASS
(Type 22) Batch 3

Ship	Pennant Number	Completion Date	Builder
CUMBERLAND	F85	1988	Yarrow
CAMPBELTOWN	F86	1988	C. Laird
CHATHAM	F87	1989	Swan Hunter
CORNWALL	F99	1987	Yarrow

Displacement 4,200 tons **Dimensions** 147m x 15m x 7m **Speed** 30 knots **Armament** 1 - 4.5" gun, 1 - Goalkeeper, 8 - Harpoon, 2 - Seawolf, 4 - 30mm guns, 6 Torpedo Tubes, 2 Lynx or 1 Sea King Helicopter **Complement** 250.

Notes
General purpose gun and Goalkeeper system added to these ships as a direct result of lessons learned during Falklands conflict. All these ships have a major anti-submarine capability. Cost £180 million each.

HMS Richmond

DUKE CLASS (Type 23)

Ship	Pennant Number	Completion Date	Builder
GRAFTON	F80	1996	Yarrow
SUTHERLAND	F81	1997	Yarrow
SOMERSET	F82	1996	Yarrow
LANCASTER	F229	1991	Yarrow
NORFOLK	F230	1989	Yarrow
ARGYLL	F231	1991	Yarrow
MARLBOROUGH	F233	1991	Swan Hunter
IRON DUKE	F234	1992	Yarrow
MONMOUTH	F235	1993	Yarrow
MONTROSE	F236	1993	Yarrow
WESTMINSTER	F237	1993	Swan Hunter
NORTHUMBERLAND	F238	1994	Swan Hunter
RICHMOND	F239	1994	Swan Hunter

Displacement 3,500 tons **Dimensions** 133m x 15m x 5m **Speed** 28 knots **Armament** Harpoon & Seawolf missile systems: 1 - 4.5" gun, 4 - 2 twin, magazine launched, Torpedo Tubes **Complement** 157.

Notes
An order was placed in 1996 for three more vessels.to be named PORTLAND(1999) KENT (2000) and ST ALBANS (2001). Delivery dates in brackets. No further orders are now likely to be placed

OFFICIAL PHOTO

HMS Ledbury

24

MINE COUNTERMEASURES SHIPS (MCMV'S) HUNT CLASS

Ship	Pennant Number	Completion Date	Builder
BRECON	M29	1980	Vosper T.
LEDBURY	M30	1981	Vosper T.
CATTISTOCK	M31	1982	Vosper T.
COTTESMORE	M32	1983	Yarrow
BROCKLESBY	M33	1983	Vosper T.
MIDDLETON	M34	1984	Yarrow
DULVERTON	M35	1983	Vosper T.
BICESTER	M36	1986	Vosper T.
CHIDDINGFOLD	M37	1984	Vosper T.
ATHERSTONE	M38	1987	Vosper T.
HURWORTH	M39	1985	Vosper T.
BERKELEY	M40	1988	Vosper T.
QUORN	M41	1989	Vosper T.

Displacement 625 tonnes **Dimensions** 60m x 10m x 2.2m **Speed** 17 knots **Armament** 1 x 30mm + 2 x 20mm guns **Complement** 45.

Notes

The largest warships ever built of glass reinforced plastic. Their cost (£35m each) has dictated the size of the class. Very sophisticated ships – and lively seaboats! All based at Portsmouth and Faslane. Ships are frequently deployed in the Fishery Protection role and from 1998 will replace the River Class in the Northern Ireland squadron.

HMS Arun

FLEET MINESWEEPERS
RIVER CLASS

Ship	Pennant Number	Completion Date	Builder
BLACKWATER	M2008	1985	Richards
ITCHEN	M2009	1985	Richards
ORWELL	M2011	1985	Richards
SPEY	M2013	1985	Richards
ARUN	M2014	1986	Richards

Displacement 850 tonnes **Dimensions** 47m x 10m x 3m **Speed** 14 knots **Armament** 1 - 40mm + 2 - GPMG **Complement** 30.

Notes

MCM ships built for service with the RNR. All were withdrawn during 1994 as a result of the 1993 defence economies. All are employed in the Northern Ireland Squadron (without pennant numbers) except ORWELL which is a training ship attached to BRNC Dartmouth.

● DANE MURDOCH

HMS Sandown

SANDOWN CLASS

Ship	Pennant Number	Completion Date	Builder
SANDOWN	M101	1989	Vosper T.
INVERNESS	M102	1991	Vosper T.
CROMER	M103	1991	Vosper T.
WALNEY	M104	1992	Vosper T.
BRIDPORT	M105	1993	Vosper T.

Displacement 450 tons **Dimensions** 53m x 10m x 2m **Speed** 13 knots **Armament** 1 - 30mm gun **Complement** 34.

Notes
A class dedicated to a single mine hunting role. Propulsion is by vectored thrust and bow thrusters. Up to 15 more ships were planned, but the 7 due to be ordered in 1991 were postponed until 1994. They will be named (acceptance dates in brackets) PENZANCE (97), PEMBROKE (98), GRIMSBY (99), BANGOR (00), RAMSEY (00), BLYTH (01), SHOREHAM (01)

27

● D HANNAFORD

HMS Dumbarton Castle

CASTLE CLASS

Ship	Pennant Number	Completion Date	Builder
LEEDS CASTLE	P258	1981	Hall Russell
DUMBARTON CASTLE	P265	1982	Hall Russell

Displacement 1,450 tons **Dimensions** 81m x 11m x 3m **Speed** 20 knots **Armament** 1 - 40mm gun **Complement** 40

Notes

These ships have a dual role – that of fishery protection and offshore patrols within the limits of UK territorial waters. Unlike the Island Class these ships are able to operate helicopters – including Sea King aircraft. Trials have been conducted to assess the suitability of these ships as Minelayers. LEEDS CASTLE is on long term deployment to the Falkland Islands with her ships' company rotating every four months.

28

● L/AIR C LEASKE

HMS Lindisfarne

ISLAND CLASS

Ship	Pennant Number	Completion Date	Builder
ANGLESEY	P277	1979	Hall Russell
ALDERNEY	P278	1979	Hall Russell
GUERNSEY	P297	1977	Hall Russell
SHETLAND	P298	1977	Hall Russell
ORKNEY	P299	1977	Hall Russell
LINDISFARNE	P300	1978	Hall Russell

Displacement 1,250 tons **Dimensions** 60m x 11m x 4m **Speed** 17 knots **Armament** 1 - 40mm gun **Complement** 39.

Notes
Built on trawler lines these ships were introduced to protect the extensive British interests in North Sea oil/gas installations and to patrol the 200 mile fishery limit. All vessels have extra crew members to allow leave to be taken and thus extend vessels time on task over the year.

HMS Peacock

PEACOCK CLASS

Ship	Pennant Number	Completion Date	Builder
PEACOCK	P239	1983	Hall Russell
PLOVER	P240	1983	Hall Russell
STARLING	P241	1984	Hall Russell

Displacement 700 tons **Dimensions** 60m x 10m x 5m **Speed** 28 knots **Armament** 1 - 76mm gun **Complement** 31.

Notes

Used to provide an ocean going back-up to the Marine Department of the Hong Kong Police. The Government of Hong Kong paid 75% of the building and maintenance costs of these vessels. Sister ships SWALLOW and SWIFT returned to UK in 1988 and were sold (Oct 88) to the Irish Navy after only 3 years RN service. All three vessels will remain in Hong Kong until the withdrawal in July 1997. Despite a UK requirement in the Fishery Protection Squadron they will be sold - possibly to the Phillipines.

HMS Archer

COASTAL TRAINING CRAFT
ARCHER CLASS

Ship	Pennant Number	Completion Date	Builder
ARCHER	P264	1985	Watercraft
BITER	P270	1985	Watercraft
SMITER	P272	1986	Watercraft
PURSUER	P273	1988	Vosper
BLAZER	P279	1988	Vosper
DASHER	P280	1988	Vosper
PUNCHER	P291	1988	Vosper
CHARGER	P292	1988	Vosper
RANGER	P293	1988	Vosper
TRUMPETER	P294	1988	Vosper

Displacement 43 tonnes **Dimensions** 20m x 6m x 1m **Speed** 20 knots **Armament** Nil
Complement 14.

Notes

In service with RN University units. TRUMPETER and RANGER deployed to Gibraltar
in 1991.

31

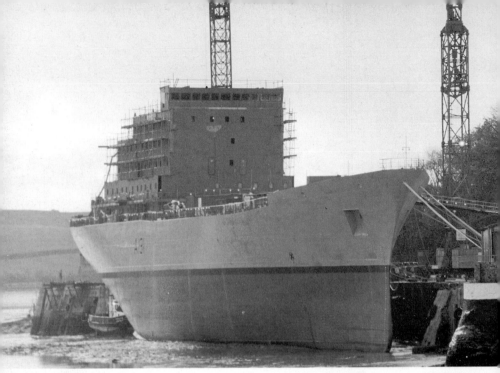

● L/AIR ANDY WHITE

SCOTT CLASS

Ship	Pennant Number	Completion Date	Builder
SCOTT	A 131	1997	Appledore

Displacement 13,300 tonnes **Dimensions** 130m x 21.5m x 14m **Speed** 17 knots **Complement** 65

Notes

Ordered in January 1995 from BAeSEMA - the first prime contract for a new ship to be placed by MoD with a firm other than a shipbuilder. Due for handover in May 1997 after trials. Fitted with the latest (US Navy) survey equipment and designed (and complemented) to remain at sea 300 days per year. SCOTT is the first RN vessel capable of being designated a Commercial Managed Fleet Auxiliary (CMFA) for operation by a civilian crew with a naval survey party embarked. Initially, the vessel will operate with a naval ships company.

HMS Roebuck

ROEBUCK CLASS

Ship	Pennant Number	Completion Date	Builder
ROEBUCK	A130	1986	Brooke Marine

Displacement 1500 tonnes **Dimensions** 64m x 13m x 4m **Speed** 15 knots **Complement** 47.

Notes
Fitted with the latest fixing aids and sector scanning sonar. An order for new vessels to replace ROEBUCK and BEAGLE/BULLDOG was expected during 1996 but the tendering exercise (only) is now expected in 1997.

● D HANNAFORD

HMS Herald

HECLA CLASS

Ship	Pennant Number	Completion Date	Builder
HERALD	A138	1974	Robb Caledon

Displacement 2,733 tons **Dimensions** 79m x 15m x 5m **Speed** 14 knots **Complement** 115.

Notes
Able to operate for long periods away from shore support, this ship and the other vessels of the Hydrographic Fleet collect the data that is required to produce the Admiralty Charts and publications which are sold to mariners worldwide. HECLA for sale at Devonport in December 1996.

● D HANNAFORD

HMS Bulldog

BULLDOG CLASS

Ship	Pennant Number	Completion Date	Builder
BULLDOG	A317	1968	Brooke Marine
BEAGLE	A319	1968	Brooke Marine

Displacement 1,088 tons **Dimensions** 60m x 11m x 4m **Speed** 15 knots
Complement 39.

Notes

Designed to operate in coastal waters. Both have been extensively refitted to extend hull life. Both due for replacement - an order for design studies is now expected in 1997. GLEANER (A86) is a small inshore survey craft based at Portsmouth.

● OFFICIAL PHOTO

HMY Britannia

ROYAL YACHT

Ship	Pennant Number	Completion Date	Builder
BRITANNIA	A00	1954	J. Brown

Displacement 5,280 tons **Dimensions** 126m x 17m x 5m **Speed** 21 knots **Complement** 250.

Notes
Probably the best known ship in the Royal Navy, BRITANNIA was designed to be converted to a hospital ship in time of war but this conversion was not made during the Falklands or Gulf crisis and the role has now been abandoned. Due to be paid off in mid 1997 -without replacement.

HMS Endurance

ICE PATROL SHIP

Ship	Pennant Number	Completion Date	Builder
ENDURANCE	A171	1990	Ulstein-Hatlo

Displacement 5,129 tons **Dimensions** 91m x 17.9m x 6.5m **Speed** 14.9 knots **Armament** Small arms **Aircraft** 2 Lynx **Complement** 113.

Notes
Chartered for only 7 months in late 1991 to replace the older vessel of the same name. Originally M/V POLAR CIRCLE, renamed HMS POLAR CIRCLE (A176) and then purchased by MOD(N) and renamed again in October 1992 to current name.

Loyal Chancellor

LOYAL CLASS

Ship	Pennant Number	Ship	Pennant Number
LOYAL WATCHER	A159	LOYAL CHANCELLOR	A1770

G.R.T. 112 tons **Dimensions** 24m x 6m x 3m **Speed** 10.5 knots **Complement** 24.

Notes
Former RNXS craft now used by the RN university units at Oxford and Cambridge.

Example

COASTAL TRAINING CRAFT
EXAMPLE CLASS

Ship	Pennant Number	Completion Date	Builder
EXPRESS	A163	1988	Vosper T
EXPLORER	A164	1985	Watercraft
EXAMPLE	A165	1985	Watercraft
EXPLOIT	A167	1988	Vosper T

Displacement 43 tons **Dimensions** 20m x 6m x 1m **Speed** 20 knots **Armament** Nil
Complement 14

Notes
Training vessels for the RNXS - until the organisation was disbanded on 31March 1994. Vessels were then transferred to RN University Units as sea training tenders.

Northella

Ship	Pennant Number	Completion Date	Builder
NORTHELLA		1973	Clelands

G.R.T. 1,535 **Dimensions** 77m x 12.7m x 6m **Speed** 15 knots **Complement** 14

Notes
Former deep water stern trawler owned by Marr's of Hull. Taken up from trade for the Falklands Conflict in 1982 (as a minesweeper) and again in 1983 as a target vessel. In 1985 again chartered for service as a Navigational Training Vessel. Charters have been renewed since then and vessel has been successfully used in a number of secondary roles. A decision was awaited in Nov 96 regarding a further extension of her charter. Can carry up to 20 trainees.

Colonel Templer

Ship	Pennant Number	Completion Date	Builder
COLONEL TEMPLER		1966	Hall Russell

Displacement 1,300 tons **Dimensions** 56m x 11m x 5.6 m **Speed** 12 knots
Complement 14

Notes

Built as a stern trawler but converted in 1980 for use by the Defence Research Agency as an acoustic research vessel. A major rebuild was completed after a serious fire gutted the ship in 1990. 12 scientists can be carried. Operated by contractors.

A number of merchant ships are on charter to various MOD departments. They include MAERSK GANNET, MAERSK ASCENCION, ST BRANDAN, INDOMITABLE and OIL MARINER in support of the Falkland Island commitment. PROUD SEAHORSE and MARINE EXPLORER have hydrographic roles in UK waters.

THE ROYAL FLEET AUXILIARY

The Royal Fleet Auxiliary Service (RFA) is a civilian manned fleet owned and operated by the Ministry of Defence. Its main task is to supply warships of the Royal Navy at sea with fuel, food, stores and ammunition which they need to remain operational while away from base.The service also provides aviation support and training facilities for the Royal Navy – together with amphibious support and secure sea transport for army units. NATO warships are frequent "customers" too (on a repayment basis).

The service prides itself that each ship is available for operations for approximately 80% of the year. Unlike the RN, officers and men of the RFA join a vessel for a period of time - say six months - and do not expect to be in port for leave periods at all during this period. In due course they are themselves relieved on board before heading home for a (lengthy) period of leave and eventually another ship. This practice of course ensures that the RFA's ships can be used to the maximum and are not seen spending weeks alongside in a base with their crew on leave.- as frequently happens to an RN ship. (This practice would hardly work on a "High Tech" RN ship where pre-joining training, work up etc would make such a rapid turn round of trained personnel at sea simply inefficient)

Throughout 1996 the service had a standing commitment to provide tankers, carrying the ever vital fuel, in the West Indies, Falklands, Gulf and Adriatic. The reduction of the commitment in the Adriatic during 1996 eased the problem for the Tankers in the fleet - there being too few vessels to meet the commitments. As can be seen from the following pages to provide this level of service with the number of operational hulls available - and fulfil training and exercise requirements too - is not easy. The basic problem which will exist for many years (unless some drastic cost cutting is carried out) is that the RFA fleet consists of some huge, labour intensive vessels which were built to support group deployments of a sizeable RN fleet from past years. The latter having been reduced considerably, leaves the RFA supporting a much smaller fleet with their huge vessels which can only be in one area at a time - leaving some operations/exercises with inadequate or zero RFA support.

SHIPS OF THE ROYAL FLEET AUXILIARY
Pennant Numbers

Ship	Pennant Number	Ship	Pennant Number	Ship	Pennant Number
BRAMBLELEAF	A81	ARGUS	A135	RESOURCE	A480
SEA CRUSADER	A96	GREY ROVER	A269	SIR BEDIVERE	L3004
BAYLEAF	A109	GOLD ROVER	A271	SIR GALAHAD	L3005
ORANGELEAF	A110	BLACK ROVER	A273	SIR GERAINT	L3027
OAKLEAF	A111	FORT GRANGE	A385	SIR PERCIVALE	L3036
OLWEN	A122	FORT AUSTIN	A386	SIR TRISTRAM	L3505
OLNA	A123	FORT VICTORIA	A387		
DILIGENCE	A132	FORT GEORGE	A388		

RFA Olwen

'OL' CLASS

Ship	Pennant Number	Completion Date	Builder
OLWEN	A122	1965	Hawthorn Leslie
OLNA	A123	1966	Hawthorn Leslie

Displacement 36,000 tons **Dimensions** 197m x 26m x 10m **Speed** 19 knots **Complement** 92.

Notes

These ships can operate up to 3 Sea King helicopters. Have been used for Helicopter training when ARGUS is not available. Dry stores can be carried – and transferred at sea – as well as a wide range of fuel, aviation spirit and lubricants. Both due to be replaced in 2000/01. A contract for new vessels was expected to be placed in December 1996.

● D HANNAFORD

RFA Black Rover

ROVER CLASS

Ship	Pennant Number	Completion Date	Builder
GREY ROVER	A269	1970	Swan Hunter
GOLD ROVER	A271	1974	Swan Hunter
BLACK ROVER	A273	1974	Swan Hunter

Displacement 11,522 tons **Dimensions** 141m x 19m x 7m **Speed** 18 knots **Armament** 2 - 20mm guns **Complement** 49/54

Notes
Small Fleet Tankers designed to supply HM ships with fresh water, dry cargo and refrigerated provisions as well as a range of fuel and lubricants. Helicopter deck but no hangar. GREY ROVER due for disposal in March 1997 but may continue in service.

● D HANNAFORD

LEAF CLASS

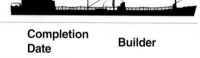

Ship	Pennant Number	Completion Date	Builder
BRAMBLELEAF	A81	1980	Cammell Laird
BAYLEAF	A109	1982	Cammell Laird
ORANGELEAF	A110	1982	Cammell Laird
OAKLEAF	A111	1981	Uddevalla V

Displacement 37,747 tons **Dimensions** 170m x 26m x 12m **Speed** 14.5 knots **Complement** 60.

Notes
All are ex merchant ships & are.mainly employed on freighting duties BRAMBLELEAF is owned by MOD (N), the remainder are on charter. OAKLEAF differs from the other ships of the class which are all commercial Stat 32 tankers. At 49,310 tons she is the largest vessel in RFA/RN service. APPLELEAF taken over by the Royal Australian Navy (as HMAS Westralia) in late 1989.

45

● OFFICIAL PHOTO

RFA Fort Grange

FORT CLASS I

Ship	Pennant Number	Completion Date	Builder
FORT GRANGE	A385	1978	Scott Lithgow
FORT AUSTIN	A386	1979	Scott Lithgow

Displacement 23,384 tons **Dimensions** 183m x 24m x 9m **Speed** 20 knots **Complement** 201, (120 RFA, 36 RNSTS & 45 RN).

Notes

Full hangar and maintenance facilities are provided and up to four Sea King helicopters can be carried for both the transfer of stores and anti-submarine protection of a group of ships. Both ships can be armed with 4 - 20mm guns mounted on the Scot platforms.

46

RFA Fort George

FORT CLASS II

Ship	Pennant Number	Completion Date	Builder
FORT VICTORIA	A387	1992	Harland & Wolff
FORT GEORGE	A388	1993	Swan Hunter

Displacement 31,500 tons **Dimensions** 204m x 30m x 9m **Speed** 20 knots **Armament** 4 - 30mm guns, Sea Wolf Missile System (Fitted for but not with) **Complement** 100 (RFA), 24 civilians, 32 RN and up to 122 aircrew.

Notes

"One stop" replenishment ships with the widest range of armaments, fuel and spares carried.Can operate up to 5 Sea King Helicopters with full maintenance facilities onboard. Both vessels eventually entered service after a series of delays in 1994. Flight deck facilities frequently used as training area for helicopter crews.

47

RFA Resource

REGENT CLASS

Ship	Pennant Number	Completion Date	Builder
RESOURCE	A480	1967	Scotts

Displacement 23,256 tons **Dimensions** 195m x 24m x 8m **Speed** 21 knots **Armament** 2 - 20mm guns **Complement** 160, (RFA 112, RNSTS 37, RN 11).

Notes
The widest range of naval armament stores are carried onboard plus a limited range of general naval stores and food. RESOURCE reverted to Reserve (Preservation by Operation) status at Rosyth in November 1991 but brought forward in late 1992 for service in the Adriatic. She has remained at Split supporting the Army in Bosnia throughout 1993/6 returning to UK for a brief refit in 1994. Was expected to return to UK and "extended readiness" during 1996 but this has been delayed until at least March 1997.

HMS Gloucester

HM Ships Sceptre
and Marlborough

F233

50

HMS Brave

HMS Richmond

M38

HMS Orwell

M2011

HMS Leeds Castle

55

RFA Argus

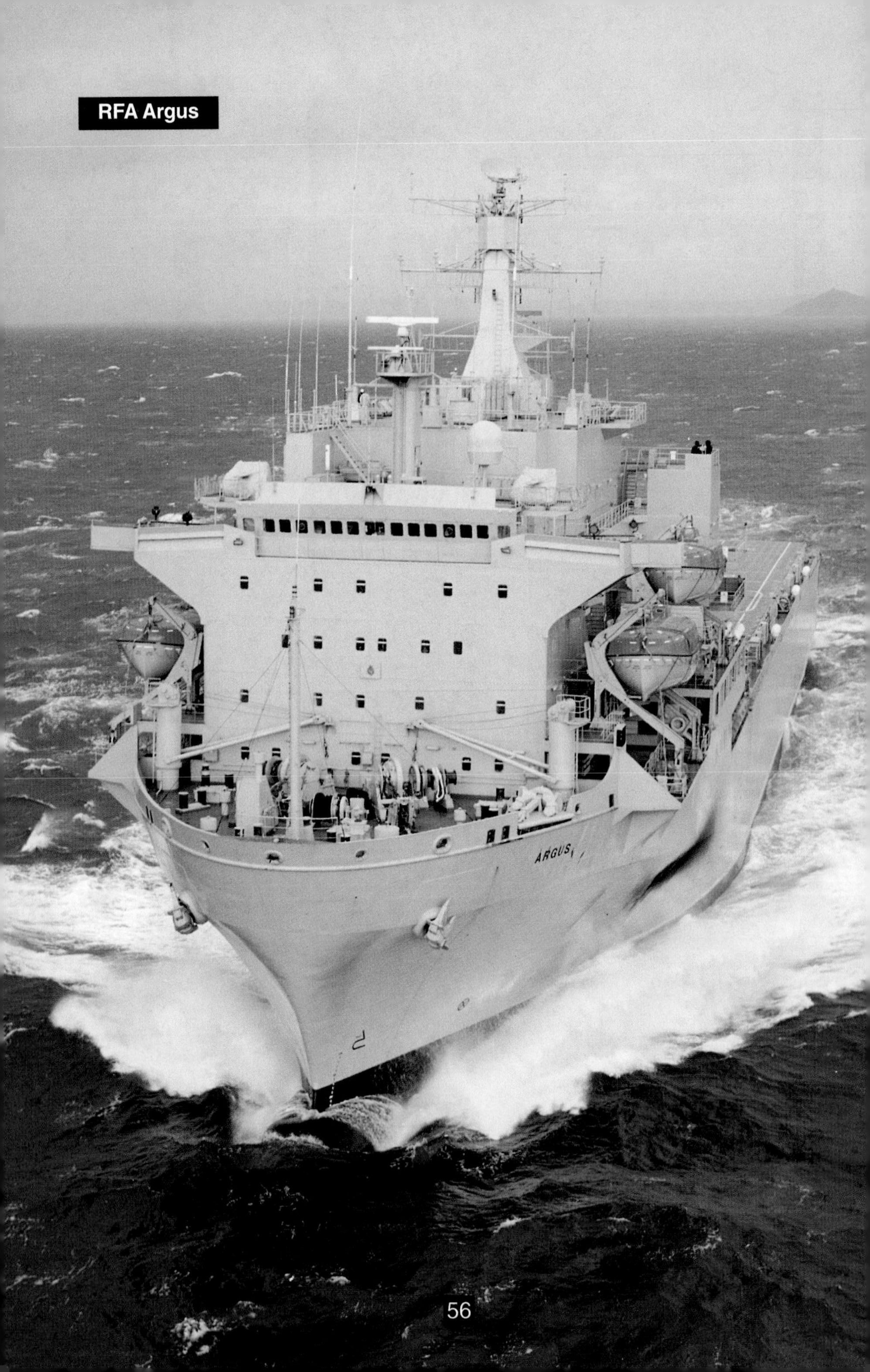

● OFFICIAL PHOTO

RFA Sir Galahad

LANDING SHIPS (LOGISTIC)
SIR LANCELOT CLASS

Ship	Pennant Number	Completion Date	Builder
SIR BEDIVERE	L3004	1967	Hawthorn
SIR GALAHAD	L3005	1987	Swan Hunter
SIR GERAINT	L3027	1967	Stephen
SIR PERCIVALE	L3036	1968	Hawthorn
SIR TRISTRAM	L3505	1967	Hawthorn

Displacement 5,550 tons **Dimensions** 126m x 18m x 4m **Speed** 17 knots **Armament** Can be fitted with 20 or 40mm guns in emergency **Complement** 65, (SIR GALAHAD is larger at 8,451 tons. 140m x 20m **Complement** 58).

Notes
Manned by the RFA but tasked by the Army, these ships are used for heavy secure transport of stores – embarked by bow and stern doors – and beach assault landings. Can operate helicopters from both vehicle and flight deck if required-and carry 340 troops. SIR TRISTRAM was rebuilt after extensive Falklands War damage. SIR BEDIVERE is now expected to complete a Ship Life Extension Programme (SLEP) at Rosyth in mid1997 which will see the vessel lengthened and considerably updated. SIR GERAINT is expected to be similarly re-built

57

● JOHN HITCHINGS

RFA Sea Crusader

Ship	Pennant Number	Completion Date	Builder
SEA CRUSADER	A96	1996	Kawasaki Heavy Industries

Displacement 25,500 tonnes **Dimensions** 164m x 25m x 6.5m **Speed** 18 knots **Complement** 17

Notes Purchased whilst being completed from Japanese builders in 1996 and arrived in UK in November for service with the Joint Rapid Reaction Force. 2,300 lane metres of vehicle space available.Negotiations continue for a second vessel. Both will be available to deploy at short notice to any international trouble spot with a considerable quantity of heavy equipment

● D HANNAFORD

RFA Diligence

Ship	Pennant Number	Completion Date	Builder
DILIGENCE	A132	1981	Oesundsvarvet

Displacement 5,814 tons **Dimensions** 120m x 12m x 3m **Speed** 15 knots **Armament** 2 - 20mm **Complement** RFA 40, RN Personnel – approx 100.

Notes
Formerly the M/V STENA INSPECTOR purchased (£25m) for service in the South Atlantic. Her deep diving complex was removed and workshops added. Has given valuable support to a wide range of warships in the Falklands and Gulf.

ARGUS

Ship	Pennant Number	Completion Date	Builder
ARGUS	A135	1981	Cantieri Navali Breda

Displacement 28,081 tons (full load) **Dimensions** 175m x 30m x 8m **Speed** 18 knots
Armament 4 - 30 mm, 2 - 20 mm **Complement** 254 (inc 137 Air Group) **Aircraft** 6 Sea King, 12 Harriers can be carried in a "ferry role".

Notes
Formerly the M/V CONTENDER BEZANT taken up from trade during the Falklands crisis. Purchased in 1984 (£13 million) for conversion to an 'Aviation Training Ship'. A £50 million re-build was undertaken at Belfast from 1984-87. Undertook rapid conversion in October 1990 to "Primary Casualty Reception Ship" (Hospital Ship!) for service in the Gulf. These facilities remain "mothballed" on board for activation if required.

ROYAL MARITIME
AUXILIARY SERVICE

Ships of the RMAS, which can be seen at work in the UK Naval Bases and at Gibraltar, are easily identified by their black hulls, buff coloured superstructure and by the RMAS flag, which is a blue ensign defaced in the fly by a yellow anchor over two wavy lines.

Pennant numbers are painted only on those vessels that are normally employed outside harbour limits.

The Marine Services became a Defence Agency on 1st April 1994 and throughout 1995, in addition to delivering its normal services, the Marine Services organisation was involved in a much discussed "Market Testing" exercise, as part of the Government's "Competing for Quality" initiative. This involved bidding for the three main areas of the business - in competition with industry. These were all the marine services at Portsmouth, Devonport and the Clyde; Moorings and Navigation Buoyage and Naval Armament freighting.

The result of the competition, announced in 1996, was that the main bulk of the RMAS work - all the Marine Services at the main ports - were lost to the contractors Serco Denholm of Greenock. The much smaller mooring/buoyage and armament freighting work remaining in house. The RMAS HQ at Bath was closed down during the year and a new smaller HQ established at Pembroke Dock. Twenty one RMAS vessels were sold in the twelve month period and further sales can be expected as vessels declared surplus to the RMAS and contractors requirements were laid up during 1996 and will be offered for disposal in the coming year.

The shape of things to come. Two 23 metre passenger transfer craft are currently being built for the MoD.
FBM - COWES

SHIPS OF
THE ROYAL MARITIME AUXILIARY SERVICE
Pennant Numbers

Ship	Pennant Number	Ship	Pennant Number
CAMERON	A72	SETTER	A189
MELTON	A83	JOAN	A190
MENAI	A84	HELEN	A198
MEON	A87	MYRTLE	A199
MILFORD	A91	SPANIEL	A201
FELICITY	A112	NORAH	A205
MAGNET	A114	LAMLASH	A208
LODESTONE	A115	LECHLADE	A211
CAIRN	A126	BEE	A216
TORRENT	A127	FORCEFUL	A221
DALMATIAN	A129	NIMBLE	A222
TORNADO	A140	POWERFUL	A223
TORCH	A141	ADEPT	A224
TORMENTOR	A142	BUSTLER	A225
TOREADOR	A143	CAPABLE	A226
WATERMAN	A146	CAREFUL	A227
FRANCES	A147	FAITHFUL	A228
FIONA	A148✔	COCKCHAFER	A230
FLORENCE	A149	DEXTEROUS	A231
GENEVIEVE	A150	ADAMANT	A232
GOOSANDER	A164	SHEEPDOG	A250
KITTY	A170	LADYBIRD	A253
LESLEY	A172	MEAVEY	A254
LILAH	A174	(SULTAN VENTURER)	
MARY	A175	ILCHESTER	A308
EDITH	A177	INSTOW	A309
HUSKY	A178	COLLIE	A328
MASTIFF	A180	IMPULSE	A344
SALUKI	A182	IMPETUS	A345
SALMOOR	A185	FELSTED	A348
SALMASTER	A186	ELKSTONE	A353
SALMAID	A187	EPWORTH	A355

Ship	Pennant Number	Ship	Pennant Number
DENMEAD	A363	HEADCORN	A1766
FULBECK	A365	HEVER	A1767
ROBUST	A366	HARLECH	A1768
NEWTON	A367	HAMBLEDON	A1769 ✓
WARDEN	A368	HOLMWOOD	A1772
KINTERBURY	A378	HORNING	A1773
ARROCHAR	A382	OILPRESS	Y21
APPLEBY	A383	OILWELL	Y23
CLOVELLY	A389	OILBIRD	Y25
DUNSTER	A393	OILMAN	Y26
FINTRY	A394	WATERCOURSE	Y30
GRASMERE	A402	WATERFOWL	Y31
CROMARTY	A488	MOORHEN	Y32
DORNOCH	A490	MOORFOWL	Y33
ROLLICKER	A502		

RMAS Robust

ROYSTERER CLASS

Ship	Pennant Number	Completion Date	Builder
ROBUST	A366	1974	C.D. Holmes
ROLLICKER	A502	1973	C.D. Holmes

G.R.T. 1,036 tons **Dimensions** 54m x 12m x 6m **Speed** 15 knots **Complement** 21.

Notes
ROYSTERER was sold to a Nigerian Commercial Company for further service in August 1996. The other two vessels were laid up (Portsmouth and the Clyde) during 1996 being surplus to requirements.

● H BALLARD

RMAS Impulse

IMPULSE CLASS

Ship	Pennant Number	Completion Date	Builder
IMPULSE	A344	1993	Dunston
IMPETUS	A345	1993	Dunston

G.R.T. 400 tons approx **Dimensions** 33m x 10m x 4m **Speed** 12 knots **Complement** 5.

Notes
Completed in 1993 specifically to serve as berthing tugs for the Trident Class submarines at Faslane.Both operated under contract by Serco Denholm.

RMAS Faithful

HARBOUR TUGS
TWIN UNIT TRACTOR TUGS (TUTT'S)

Ship	Pennant Number	Completion Date	Builder
FORCEFUL	A221	1985	R. Dunston
NIMBLE	A222	1985	R. Dunston
POWERFUL	A223	1985	R. Dunston
ADEPT	A224	1980	R. Dunston
BUSTLER	A225	1981	R. Dunston
CAPABLE	A226	1981	R. Dunston
CAREFUL	A227	1982	R. Dunston
FAITHFUL	A228	1985	R. Dunston
DEXTEROUS	A231	1986	R. Dunston

G.R.T. 375 tons **Dimensions** 39m x 10m x 4m **Speed** 12 knots **Complement** 9.

Notes
The principal harbour tug in naval service. All operated under contract by Serco Denholm except CAPABLE at Gibraltar which is managed locally.

66

RMAS Sheepdog

DOG CLASS

Ship	Pennant Number	Ship	Pennant Number
CAIRN ●	A126	SETTER	A189
DALMATIAN	A129	SPANIEL	A201
HUSKY	A178	SHEEPDOG	A250
MASTIFF	A180	COLLIE ●	A328
SALUKI	A182		

G.R.T. 152 tons **Dimensions** 29m x 8m x 4m **Speed** 12 knots **Complement** 5.

Notes

General harbour tugs – all completed between 1965 and 1969. All except those marked ● are operated by Serco Denholm. COLLIE and CAIRN are no longer tugs but are classified as trials vessels - based at Kyle of Lochalsh.

DEERHOUND and ELKHOUND sold to Babcock at Rosyth Royal Dockyard. SEALY-HAM sold locally at Gibraltar and BASSET to Portland Port during 1996.

RMAS Joan

TRITON CLASS

Ship	Pennant Number		Ship	Pennant Number
KITTY	A170		JOAN	A190
LESLEY	A172		MYRTLE	A199
LILAH	A174		NORAH	A205
MARY	A175			

G.R.T. 89 tons **Speed** 8 knots **Complement** 4.

Notes
Known as Water Tractors these craft are used for basin moves and towage of light barges. IRENE, ISABEL, NANCY, JOYCE and KATHLEEN sold during 1996.

RMAS Fiona

FELICITY CLASS

Ship	Pennant Number		Ship	Pennant Number
FELICITY	A112		FLORENCE	A149
FRANCES	A147		GENEVIEVE	A150
FIONA	A148		HELEN	A198

G.R.T. 80 tons **Speed** 10 knots **Complement** 4.

Notes

Water Tractors used for the movement of small barges and equipment. All are operated by Serco Denholm. Two sister vessels (GEORGINA and GWENDOLINE) sold to
Serco Denholm in 1996 for service in H M Naval bases. (Both now painted red/pink).

RMAS Newton

RESEARCH VESSEL

Ship	Pennant Number	Completion Date	Builder
NEWTON	A367	1976	Scotts

G.R.T. 2,779 tons **Dimensions** 99m x 16m x 6m **Speed** 15 knots **Complement** 39

Notes
An underwater research vessel with a limited cable laying capability. Employed by the Defence Research Agency. Operated by the RMAS.

RMAS Arrochar

ARMAMENT STORES CARRIERS

Ship	Pennant Number	Completion Date	Builder
KINTERBURY	A378	1981	Appledore SB
ARROCHAR	A382	1981	Appledore SB

G.R.T. 1,357 tons **Dimensions** 64m x 12m x 5m **Speed** 14 knots **Complement** 19.

Notes
2 holds carry Naval armament stores, ammunition and guided missiles. Both vessels vary slightly. ARROCHAR (ex ST GEORGE) taken over in late 1988 from the Army. Both vessels continue to be operated by the RMAS.

● CHRIS HOCKADAY

RMAS Ladybird

INSECT CLASS

Ship	Pennant Number	Completion Date	Builder
BEE	A216	1970	C.D. Holmes
COCKCHAFER	A230	1973	Beverley
LADYBIRD	A253	1973	Beverley

G.R.T. 279 tons **Dimensions** 34m x 8m x 3m **Speed** 10.5 knots **Complement** 7-9.

Notes
COCKCHAFER is fitted as a Trials Stores Carrier and operated by the RMAS. Remainder are Naval Armament carriers and operated by Serco Denholm. SCARAB and CICALA sold during 1996

RMAS Adamant

ADAMANT

Ship	Pennant Number	Completion Date	Builder
ADAMANT	A232	1992	FBM (Cowes)

GRT 170 tonnes **Dimensions** 30m x 8m x 1m **Speed** 22 knots **Complement** 5

Notes
Twin catamaran hulls based on the commercial Red Jet design (as used by Red Funnel Ferry Co). First water jet propulsion vessel owned by MoD(N). In service as a Clyde personnel ferry - operated by Serco Denholm.

● DANE MURDOCH

RMAS Meon

(TYPE A, B & X) TENDERS

Ship	Pennant Number	Ship	Pennant Number
MELTON	A83	FULBECK §	A365
MENAI	A84	DUNSTER	A393
MEON	A87	FINTRY §	A394
MILFORD	A91	GRASMERE	A402
LAMLASH	A208	DORNOCH §	A490
LECHLADE	A211	HEADCORN	A1766
ILCHESTER ●	A308	HEAVER	A1767
INSTOW ●	A309	HARLECH	A1768
FELSTED §	A348	HAMBLEDON	A1769
ELKSTONE	A353	HOLMWOOD	A1772
EPWORTH	A355	HORNING	A1773

G.R.T. 78 tons **Dimensions** 24m x 6m x 3m **Speed** 10.5 knots **Complement** 4/5.

Notes

Vessels marked ● are diving tenders. Remainder are Training Tenders, Passenger Ferries, or Cargo Vessels. MEAVEY (A254) operates for HMS SULTAN as SULTAN VENTURER. LLANDOVERY, LYDFORD, LOYAL HELPER, SUPPORTER and CRICKLADE sold during 1996. All except MELTON are operated by Serco Denholm. Those marked § are surplus to requirements. DUNSTER in reserve.

● DANE ,MURDOCH

RMAS Oilpress

COASTAL OILERS
OILPRESS CLASS

Ship	Pennant Number	Completion Date	Builder
OILPRESS	Y21	1969	Appledore Shipbuilders
OILWELL	Y23	1969	Appledore Shipbuilders
OILBIRD	Y25	1969	Appledore Shipbuilders
OILMAN	Y26	1969	Appledore Shipbuilders

G.R.T. 362 tons **Dimensions** 41m x 9m x 3m **Speed** 11 knots **Complement** 5.

Notes
Employed as Harbour and Coastal Oilers. Only OILMAN in service (Operated by Serco Denholm) remainder are laid up being surplus to requirements.

RMAS Waterman

WATER CARRIERS
WATER CLASS

Ship	Pennant Number	Completion Date	Builder
WATERCOURSE	Y30	1974	Drypool Eng Co
WATERFOWL	Y31	1974	Drypool Eng Co
WATERMAN	A146	1978	R. Dunston

G.R.T. 263 tons **Dimensions** 40m x 8m x 2m **Speed** 11 knots **Complement** 5.

Notes

Capable of coastal passages, these craft normally supply either demineralised or fresh water to the Fleet within port limits. WATERSPOUT sold 1996. WATERCOURSE operated by Serco Denholm remainder are laid up surplus to requirements.

RMAS Lodestone

DEGAUSSING VESSELS
MAGNET CLASS

Ship	Pennant Number	Completion Date	Builder
MAGNET	A114	1979	Cleland
LODESTONE	A115	1980	Cleland

G.R.T. 828 tons **Dimensions** 55m x 12m x 4m **Speed** 14 knots **Complement** 9.

Notes
LODESTONE is laid up as surplus to requirements (Clyde). MAGNET is based at Portsmouth operated by the RMAS.

● C. HOCKADAY

RMAS Torrent

TORPEDO RECOVERY VESSELS (TRV'S) TORRID CLASS

Ship	Pennant Number	Completion Date	Builder
TORRENT	A127	1971	Cleland SB Co

G.R.T. 550 tons **Dimensions** 46m x 9m x 3m **Speed** 12 knots **Complement** 14.

Notes
A stern ramp is built for the recovery of torpedoes fired for trials and exercises. A total of 32 can be carried. Operated by the RMAS at Kyle of Lochalsh.

● D HANNAFORD

RMAS Tormentor

TORNADO CLASS

Ship	Pennant Number	Completion Date	Builder
TORNADO	A140	1979	Hall Russell
TORCH	A141	1980	Hall Russell
TORMENTOR	A142	1980	Hall Russell
TOREADOR	A143	1980	Hall Russell

G.R.T. 560 tons **Dimensions** 47m x 8m x 3m **Speed** 14 knots **Complement** 13.

Notes
All vessels have had suitable rails fitted to enable them to operate as exercise minelayers in addition to their torpedo recovery role. TORCH in reserve - future undecided. TOREADOR is surplus to requirements.

● W SARTORI

RMAS Salmoor

MOORING & SALVAGE VESSELS
SAL CLASS

Ship	Pennant Number	Completion Date	Builder
SALMOOR	A185	1985	Hall Russell
SALMASTER	A186	1986	Hall Russell
SALMAID	A187	1986	Hall Russell

Displacement 2200 tonnes **Dimensions** 77m x 15m x 4m **Speed** 15 knots **Complement** 17.

Notes
Multi-purpose vessels designed to lay and maintain underwater targets and moorings and undertake a wide range of salvage tasks. SALMASTER operated by Serco Denholm. GOOSANDER laid up Surplus to Requirements at Portsmouth.

RMAS Cameron

MOOR CLASS

Ship	Pennant Number	Completion Date	Builder
MOORHEN	Y32	1989	McTay Marine
MOORFOWL	Y33	1989	McTay Marine
CAMERON	A72	1991	Richard Dunston

Displacement 518 tons **Dimensions** 32m x 11m x 2m **Speed** 8 knots **Complement** 10

Notes
Powered mooring lighters for use within sheltered coastal waters. CAMERON is similar but was sold to Defence Research Agency (Dunfermline) in 1996 and is employed as an Underwater Trials & Experimental vessel at Rosyth. Operated under local contract.

● W SARTORI

RMAS Warden

WARDEN CLASS

Ship	Pennant Number	Completion Date	Builder
WARDEN	A368	1989	Richards

Displacement 626 tons **Dimensions** 48m x 10m x 4m **Speed** 15 knots **Complement** 11.

Notes
Range Maintenance Vessel working on the RAE Aberporth range (S. Wales). Based at Devonport from 1996 and operated by Serco Denholm. Fitted with 30 tonne bollard pull towing winch to provide alternative employment for her.

The Deputy Director of Marine Services Support (DDMSS) is responsible for the provision of marine services & support for both RAF training and range safety/clearance duties at Army and MoD ranges throughout Britain. Such services are currently delivered under two separate Government Owned/Commercially Operated (GO/CO) contracts. Management of the contracts and overall provision of the service remains the responsibility of DDMSS.

The primary tasks for RAF Support craft include target towing, winch training helicopter crews for SAR and the vessels are also used for sea survival training of aircrew. Details of RAF Support Craft are as follows: (All vessels on this page are operated under contract by GFE AV Seawork)

LONG RANGE RECOVERY AND SUPPORT CRAFT (LRRSC)

Ship	Pennant Number	Completion Date	Builder
SEAL	5000	1967	Brooke Marine
SEAGULL	5001	1970	Fairmile Const.

G.R.T. 251 tons **Dimensions** 36.6m x 7.16mx 1.8m **Speed** 21 knots **Complement** 8. Both are based at Invergordon.

RESCUE AND TARGET TOWING LAUNCHES (RTTL)

SPITFIRE, HALIFAX, HAMPDEN, HURRICANE, LANCASTER & WELLINGTON

G.R.T. 60 tons **Dimensions** 24m x 5.6m x 1.6m **Speed** 21 knots **Complement** 4/6 They are based at Great Yarmouth and Plymouth.

There are also 3 x 63' Pinnaces Nos 1374, 1389 & 1392.
These 63' craft are employed on target towing, SAR training, sea survival drills & various trials and weapon recovery. They are based at Holyhead & Plymouth.

Details of Range Safety Craft are as follows:

Ship	Pennant Number	Completion Date	Builder
FALCONET	Y01	1983	James & Stone
PETARD	Y02	1978	James & Stone

G.R.T. 60 tons **Dimensions** 24m x 5.5m x 1.5m **Speed** 21 knots **Complement** 6. They are based at Benbecula and Pembroke Dock.

HMAV Ardennes

ARMY LANDING CRAFT
LCL CLASS (LANDING CRAFT LOGISTIC)

Vessel	Pennant Number	Completion Date	Builder
HMAV ARDENNES	L4001	1977	Brooke Marine
HMAV ARAKAN	L4003	1978	Brooke Marine

G.R.T. 1,595 tons **Dimensions** 72m x 15m x 2.5m **Speed** 10 knots **Complement** 36.

Notes
Designed to carry up to 520 tonnes of cargo, overside loaded, or up to Five Chieftain tanks – Ro Ro loaded, reducing to 254 tonnes for beaching operations, through bow doors. Principal roles are maintenance of the Royal Artillery Range Outer Hebrides and in support of Amphibious Operations and Exercises.

RCTV Audemer

RCL CLASS
(RAMPED CRAFT LOGISTIC)

Vessel	Pennant Number	Completion Date	Builder
RCTV ANDALSNES	L107	1984	James & Stone
RCTV AKYAB	L109	1984	James & Stone
RCTV AACHEN	L110	1986	James & Stone
RCTV AREZZO	L111	1986	James & Stone
RCTV ARROMANCHES	L112	1987	James & Stone
RCTV AUDEMER	L113	1987	James & Stone

Displacement 165 tons **Dimensions** 33m x 8m x 1.5m **Speed** 9 knots **Complement** 6.

Notes
Smaller – "all purpose" landing craft capable of carrying up to 100 tons. In service in coastal waters around Cyprus and UK. ARROMANCHES was formerly AGHEILA (re-named 1994 when original vessel was sold).

Alnmouth

SEA CADET VESSELS

FLEET TENDERS 63 DESIGN

Ship	Pennant Number	Ship	Pennant Number
ALNMOUTH	Y13	APPLEBY	A383

Displacement 117 tons **Dimensions** 24m x 5m x 3m **Speed** 10.5 knots.

Notes
'Craft are loaned by MoD to the Sea Cadet Corps and are used by units throughout the UK.from March to October each year.
ALNMOUTH and APPLEBY brought up to DTI standards and returned to service mid '94. ABERDOVEY and ABINGER sold in 1995.

Ex-BIBURY (A103) operates for Portsmouth Naval Base Sub Aqua Club.

AIRCRAFT OF THE FLEET AIR ARM

British Aerospace Sea Harrier

Variants: F/A 2
Role: Short take off, vertical landing (STOVL) fighter attack and reconnaissance aircraft.
Engine: 1 x 21,500lb thrust Rolls Royce PEGASUS 104, turbofan.
Span 25' 3" **Length** 49' 1" **Height** 12' 0" **Max weight** 26,200lb.
Max speed Mach .9 540 knots **Crew** 1 pilot.
Avionics: Blue Vixen pulse doppler radar
Armament: Up to 4 x AMRAAM Air to Air Missiles. SEA EAGLE air to surface missiles. SIDEWINDER air to air missiles. 2 - 30mm Aden cannons with 120 rounds per gun in detachable pods, one either side of the lower fuselage. 1 fuselage centreline and 4 underwing hardpoints. The inner wing stations are capable of carrying 2,000lb of stores and are plumbed for drop tanks. The other positions can carry stores up to 1,000lb in weight. Possible loads include 1,000lb or practice bombs; BL 755 cluster bombs, 190 or 100 gallon drop tanks. A single F95 camera can be mounted obliquely in the nose for reconnaissance.
Squadron Service: 800, 801 and 899 squadrons in commission.
Notes: During 1997, 800 squadron will be embarked in HMS INVINCIBLE and 801 in HMS ILLUSTRIOUS. 899 squadron is responsible for the training of pilots and maintainers and the development of tactics.It is normally shore based at Yeovilton. In a period of tension it could embark to reinforce the embarked air groups in the carriers.

OFFICIAL PHOTO

Westland SEA KING

Developed for the Royal Navy from the Sikorsky SH3D, the basic Sea King airframe is used in three different roles. The following details are common to all:
Engines: 2 x 1600shp Rolls Royce Gnome H 1400 – 1 free power turbines.
Rotor Diameter 62' 0" **Length** 54' 9" **Height** 17' 2" **Max Weight** 21,400lb **Max Speed** 125 knots.
The 3 versions are:-

OFFICIAL PHOTO

SAR MK 5 : HAS 6

The HAS6 has improved sonics, deeper dipping active sonar and ESM
Roles: Anti-submarine search and strike. SAR. Transport.
Crew: 2 pilots, 1 observer and 1 aircrewman.
Avionics: Sea Searcher radar; Type 2069 variable depth active/passive sonar AQS 902 passive sonobuoy analyser. Orange Crop passive ESM equipment.
Armament: 4 fuselage hardpoints capable of carrying STINGRAY torpedoes or depth charges. Various flares, markers, grenades and sonobuoys can be carried internally and hand launched. A 7.62mm machine gun can be mounted in the doorway.
Squadron Service: 771 Squadron operates an SAR 5.706, 810, 814, 819, and 820 squadrons are in commission equipped with HAS 6.
Notes: The Sea King has been the backbone of the Fleet Air Arm's anti-submarine force since 1970. 706 is the advanced training squadron at Culdrose. 810 is an operational flying training squadron with the capability to embark to reinforce the front line. During 1997, 814 squadron will be embarked in HMS INVINCIBLE and 820 in HMS ILLUSTRIOUS. 819 is shore based at Prestwick The SAR 5 has an excellent SAR capability which is frequently demonstrated in the south west approaches. The HAS 6 has less complete SAR facilities when full ASW equipment fitted.

AEW 2

Role: Airborne Early Warning. **Crew:** 1 pilot and 2 observers.
Avionics: Thorn/EMI Searchwater radar Orange Crop passive ESM equipment.
Squadron Service: 849 HQ, 849A and 849B flights in commission.
Notes: Used to detect low flying aircraft trying to attack aircraft carrier battle groups under conventional shipborne radar cover. Can also be used for surface search utilising its sophisticated, computerised long range radar. During 1997 849A flight will be embarked in HMS INVINCIBLE and 849B in HMS ILLUSTRIOUS 849HQ acts as a training and trials unit at Culdrose.

HC 4

Role: Commando assault and utility transport.
Crew: 2 pilots and 1 aircrewman.
Armament: Door mounted 7.62mm machine gun.
Squadron Service: 845 , 846 and 848 squadrons in commission.
Notes: The HC4 has a fixed undercarriage with no sponsons or radome.Can carrying up to 27 troops in the cabin or underslung loads up to 8,000lb in weight. All squadrons are based at Yeovilton but embark or detach at short notice to support 3 Cdo Brigade.845 Sqn has had aircraft based in Split in support of UN & NATO Forces in Bosnia since1993.

Westland LYNX

Variants: HAS 3, HAS 3S, HMA 8.
Roles: Surface search and strike; anti-submarine strike; SAR.
Engines: 2 x 900hp Rolls Royce GEM BS 360-07-26 free shaft turbines.
Rotor diameter: 42' 0" **Length** 39' 1" **Height** 11' 0" **Max Weight** 9,500lb.
Max Speed: 150 knots. **Crew:** 1 pilot and 1 observer.
Avionics: SEA SPRAY radar. Orange Crop passive ESM equipment. Sea Owl PID (Mk 8)
Armament: External pylons carry up to 4 - SEA SKUA air to surface missiles or 2 x STINGRAY, Mk 46 torpedoes, depth charges, flares or markers.
Squadron Service: 702 and 815 squadrons in commission.

Notes: 815 OEU FLT is a trials squadron with equipment for HMA 8 and 702 is a training squadron based at Portland. 815 squadron also based at Portland is the parent unit for single aircraft ships flights. A "military" version of the Lynx, the AH7 is operated by 847 NAS which is based at Yeovilton.
The HMA Mk 8 is now flying and undergoing intensive development trials. Full delivery of 44 conversions expected by 2003.

Westland GAZELLE HT2

Engine: 1 x 592shp Turbomeca ASTAZOU free power turbine.
Crew: 1 or 2 pilots.

Notes: In service with 705 squadron at Culdrose. Used for training all RN helicopter pilots up to "wings standard" before they move onto the Sea King or Lynx. A "military" version of the Gazelle, the AH1, is used by 847 NAS based at Yeovilton as a spotter/communications aircraft for the Royal Marines.

OTHER AIRCRAFT TYPES IN ROYAL NAVY SERVICE DURING 1997

British Aerospace JETSTREAM T2 and T3

Engines: 2 x 940hp Turbomeca ASTAZOU 16D turboprops. (T3 Garrett turboprops).
Crew: 1 or 2 pilots, 2 student observers plus 3 other seats.
Notes: T2's are used by 750 squadron at Culdrose for training Fleet Air Arm Observers. T3's are used by the Heron flight at Yeovilton for operational support/communications flying.

GROB G115 D-2

Has taken over the flying grading and conversion of Rotary to Fixed Wing flying task from the Chipmunk. They are owned and operated by a division of Short Brothers plc. They operate from Plymouth City Airport.

British Aerospace HAWK

Engine: 1 x Ardour Mk 151 5200 lbs thrust.
Crew: 1 or 2 Pilots (both service and civilian)
Notes: With FRADU at Culdrose to provide support for training of RN ships, RN flying standards flight and as airborne targets for the aircraft direction school.

Royal Navy Historic Flight

The RNHF is a trust which has been financially independent from the RN since 1995. It's aircraft take part in air shows throughout the UK.
The current holding of aircraft is:

Flying: 2 Fairey Swordfish, 1 Fairey Firefly (Being refurbished 97-98),1 Sea Hawk.
Static Display: 1 Fairey Swordfish
Under refurbishment at BAe Brough: 1 Hawker Sea Fury

Full details of these and many other naval aircraft can be found in the revised edition of AIRCRAFT OF THE ROYAL NAVY SINCE 1945 published by Maritime Books.

Trident II D5

The UK contribution to the NATO strategic deterrent. This submarine launched ballistic missile is 13 metres long and over 2 metres in diameter. It weighs 60 tonnes. Powered by a 3 stage solid fuel rocket motor, it has a range of 4,000 miles. Each missile is capable of delivering up to 12 warheads engaging a number of different targets.

WEAPONS OF THE ROYAL NAVY

Sea Launched Missiles

Sea Wolf

A high speed close-range anti-missile and anti-aircraft missile with fully automatic radar control and guidance. It is fitted in some frigates. A vertical launch version is fitted in the Type 23 frigates.

Sea Dart

A medium-range anti-aircraft missile with anti-ship capability. Propulsion is by ramjet and solid boost. It is carried in aircraft carriers and destroyers.

Harpoon

An anti-ship missile with low-level trajectory, radar control and guidance. Powered by turbojet it has a range of 92km. The encapsulated submarine-launched missile is already in service and a ship launched version is fitted in the latest Type 22 and Type 23 frigates.

Exocet

A medium-range anti-ship missile with a very low trajectory. Terminal guidance is by an active radar seeker. It is powered by a two stage solid propellant motor and has a range of 50km. It is fitted in some frigates.

Air Launched Missiles

Sea Skua

An anti-surface vessel missile carried by the Lynx helicopter. It has a semi-active homing seeker and a range of 20,000 metres. It is powered by solid propellant boost and sustainer motors.

Sidewinder

An infra-red homing air-to-air guided missile. It has a solid propellant motor and high explosive warhead. It is carried on the Sea Harrier and has a range of 17,700 metres.

Sea Eagle

A long-range autonomous anti-ship missile. Powered by a turbojet it has a sea-skimming flight profile and active radar guidance for terminal target acquisition. Two missiles can be carried by the Sea Harrier.

Amraam

A latest generation medium range air-to-air missile with active radar homing in the terminal phase. Powered by a solid propellent it has a range of 50km.

Guns
114m Vickers Mk8

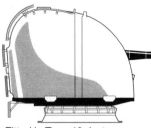

Fitted in Type 42 destroyers and the latest Type 22 and 23 frigates. Capable of firing a range of ammunition at up to 25 rounds per minute (rpm) out to a maximum range of 22km.

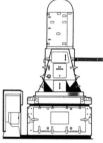

Phalanx

A 20mm automatic Gatling gun Close-In Weapon System (CIWS). Produced in the US it has a range of approximately 1 mile and a 3,000 rpm rate of fire. Fitted in Type 42, LPD and LPH.

Goalkeeper

A 30mm CIWS fitted in aircraft carriers and Type 22 Batch 3 frigates. The 7 barrelled gun can fire at the rate of 4,200 rpm.

20mm

This standard light AA gun originates from the Second World War. It has a rate of fire of 200 rpm and is fitted in many RN vessels.

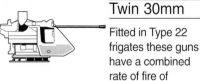

Twin 30mm

Fitted in Type 22 frigates these guns have a combined rate of fire of 1,300 rpm.

Torpedoes

Sting Ray

This lightweight torpedo embodies a number of advanced design features, is extremely robust and is capable of being launched from fixed wing aircraft, helicopters and surface ships. By virtue of its speed and manoeuvrability it can engage a wide range of targets.

Mk24 Tigerfish

One of the most advanced acoustic homing, battery driven torpedoes in the world. It is initially guided by wire but has its own homing device for the final stage of attack. It can be regarded as an underwater guided missile for use against submarines or surface ships.

Spearfish

A heavyweight torpedo, externally similar to Tigerfish in appearance, but with a turbine engine which will provide greater speed and range. Initially wire guided, its inboard computers and sonar will provide enhanced capability against the latest generation of submarines.

At the end of the line ...

Readers may well find other warships afloat which are not mentioned in this book. The majority have fulfiled a long and useful life and are now relegated to non-seagoing duties. The following list gives details of their current duties:

Pennant Number	Ship	Remarks
A134	RAME HEAD	Escort Maintenance Vessel – Royal Marines Training Ship in Fareham Creek (Portsmouth)
C35	BELFAST	World War II Cruiser Museum ship – Pool of London Open to the public daily Tel: 0171-407 6434
D23	BRISTOL	Type 82 Destroyer – Sea Cadet Training Ship at Portsmouth.
D73	CAVALIER	World War II Destroyer Museum Ship at Hebburn Not open to public. Future under consideration.
F126	PLYMOUTH	Type 12 Frigate & Oberon class Submarine Museum Ships at Birkenhead, Wirral.
S21	ONYX	Open to the public daily. Tel: 0151 650 1573
M1115	BRONINGTON	Ton Class Minesweeper at Manchester Limited Opening to the Public Tel 0161 877 7778
S67	ALLIANCE	Submarine – Museum Ship at Gosport Open to the public daily. Tel: 01705 511485
M1151	IVESTON	(Thurrock) } Static Sea
M1154	KELLINGTON	(Stockton upon Tees) } Cadet Training
M1200	SOBERTON	(Erith) } Vessels

At the time of publishing (December 1996) the following ships were awaiting tow for scrap or sale.

PORTSMOUTH
Kent   Jupiter
Scylla   Hermione
Brinton   Sheraton
Wilton

PEMBROKE DOCK
Sirius

ROSYTH
Churchill
Dreadnought
Revenge
Swiftsure
Resolution
Renown
Repulse

PLYMOUTH
Conqueror
Courageous
Warspite
Valiant
Hecla

96